MALTA
& ITS ISLANDS

MILLER

Contents

© 2015 Miller Distributors Limited.
© 2015 Text, Miller Distributors Limited.
© 2015 Photography, R. Spiteri & D. Borg @ Kuluri (except pgs 121 & 123 Għanafest Darren Zammit Lupi)

Published by Miller Distributors Limited • Design & Layout by Kuluri, www.kuluri.com.mt • Illustrations by Daniel Pantalleresco
Translation by Transcripta Translation Services.

Miller Distributors Limited,
Miller House, Tarxien Road, Airport Way, Luqa, Malta.
T: +356 2166 4488 • F: +356 2167 6799
E: info@millermalta.com • W: www.millermalta.com

INTRODUCTION

Lying 90km to the south of Sicily and 290km to the north of the African mainland, 1830km to the east of Gibraltar and 1500km to the west of Alexandria, Malta and its islands might be said to occupy a position in the centre of the Mediterranean.

The group is composed of the islands of Malta, Gozo and Comino, all of which are inhabited, and the smaller uninhabited islands of Cominotto, Filfla and St Paul. The longest distance in Malta in a south-east/north-west axis is about 27km and the widest distance is about 14km. The corresponding figures for Gozo are 14km and 7km.

The indentations around the coast form base, sandy beaches and rocky coves and, more importantly, deep natural harbours. With a population of around 400 000 crowding an area of 320km^2, the Maltese Islands can claim to form the most densely populated country in Europe.

✠ PREHISTORY

Around the year 4000B.C. a group of late Stone-age Sicilian farming families left their island home to settle in a small group of islands to the south. They brought with them their domestic animals, pottery, bags of seed and flint implements. They were the first Maltese. In time, these early Maltese increased and prospered and, over a considerable period of time they undertook the construction of temples. Around 1800B.C. the temple builders disappeared. At one time, it was believed that they succumbed to an invasion of fresh migrants who exterminated or enslaved the original settlers and took over the land.

In the case of an invasion, the new arrivals, who originally hailed from the heel of Italy, would have had no difficulty in overcoming the remnants of the original stock who had colonized the islands some 2200 years before. If the first settlers were peaceful farmers, the newcomers were more aggressive. These pasture farmers were less civilized than the folk they had replaced. They built no temples but re-used the older, copper-age, temples as cemeteries.

The bronze-age farmers were not allowed to enjoy their islands in peace, as some 600 years after their arrival a new wave of bronze-using warriors invaded the land, this time in a definite attack for conquest, and made it their home. This event took place around 1200B.C. Imitating their war-like predecessors, they established their settlements in easily defensible positions.

The last of the three ages of antiquity – the Iron Age – is represented in the Maltese Islands by the remains of a single settlement at Baħrija (circa 900B.C.).

✳ THE PHOENICIANS

The Maltese Islands, with their fine natural harbours, provided an outpost which the Phoenicians founded around 800B.C. As it was in other countries, so it was in Malta:

having gained a foothold as traders, they gradually intermarried and integrated with the bronze-age farmers.

In the case of the Maltese Islands, the Phoenicians did venture inland because their artefacts have been found in several places, even as far as Rabat in the centre of the island of Malta. The weaving industry that flourished before the arrival of the Phoenicians probably received an added boost and a wider export market. Pottery was now thrown on a wheel instead of being coiled, as was previously the case.

The links between the Phoenician colonies and their central state were never very strong and when the Phoenician homeland was overrun, it was the colony of Carthage that assumed the role of mother country. In many sectors of the Mediterranean, the Phoenicians of Carthage strove to establish a sphere of influence, their chief rivals in this respect being the Greeks. Surprisingly, in the Maltese Islands these differences did not seem to exist: it is not known how many Greeks lived, or co-existed rather, with the Phoenicians and the Carthaginians on the island, but some undoubtedly did – civic institutions that resemble the Greek counterparts, together with Greek coins and pottery have been found on the islands.

▼ Skorba Temple, Mgarr

✳ THE ROMANS

Apparently, the Roman invasion did not present great difficulties and it has been suggested that the Phoenicians on the Island turned against their Carthaginian cousins and handed over the garrison to the invading Romans. The Maltese were treated more like allies than as conquered people; they kept their traditions, their language and their gods. The Romans built the city of Melita, which took the same name as that of the island, over an older, Punic settlement in what is now the Rabat/Mdina area in Malta, as well as another town in Gozo where Victoria (Rabat) now is.

✳ SAINT PAUL

The shipwreck of St Paul in 60A.D. is recorded in the Acts of the Apostles. This, together with a Pauline tradition of long standing, supported by archaeological excavations carried out at *San Pawl Milqi,* proves beyond doubt that his arrival in Malta is a historical fact. In addition, during his three-month stay on the island he sowed the first seeds of the Christian religion to which the Maltese people overwhelmingly belong. The Apostle Paul was, at the time, being taken to Rome under arrest to be judged before Caesar, as was his right as a Roman Citizen. Among the other prisoners was the physician St Luke who recorded the account of that eventful journey.

The nearest habitation to the place of the shipwreck was the villa of Publius, the chief official of the island. All those who had been

▲ Mosaic of St Paul in Mdina

shipwrecked spent three days there and, after regaining their strength, they moved on to Melita, the main town of the island. In the city, Paul cured Publius' father of a fever, after which the Roman official converted to Christianity and was later ordained bishop by St Paul. St Publius was the first bishop of Malta. After three months, by which time the sea was once more deemed safe for navigation, St Paul sailed on to Rome and to his subsequent martyrdom.

Tradition has it that a church was built on the site of the palace of Publius, were St Paul had cured his father. Many times rebuilt, the site is now occupied by the Cathedral Church dedicated to St Paul in Mdina.

▲ Mosaic Detail found at Roman Villa, Rabat

✵ THE ARABS

The Arab attacks on the island started round the year 836, during which time Malta and its islands were still under Byzantine rule. However, the islands were only conquered in the year 870 by Aglabid Arabs originating from what is now Tunisia, who used Sicily to launch their invasion, as Sicily had been occupied by them for some thirty years previously.

To better protect their new territories, the Muslims sectioned off a part of the old Roman town of Melita and defended it with a ditch. They called this citadel Mdina, and the capital of the sister island, Gozo was also divided in the same way. The elite of the small number of Arabs then on the island probably dwelt in these towns but Arab villages were scattered on both islands.

The Arabs introduced the water-wheel, the *sienja*; an animal-driven device for raising water now practically obsolete, and, much more importantly, the cultivation of the cotton plant, the mainstay of the Maltese economy for several centuries.

✵ THE MIDDLE AGES

The Arabs in Sicily were divided, and taking advantage of the situation, Count Roger the Norman, after a series of campaigns, brought the island under Norman Rule. Count Roger had invaded the islands to make sure his southern flank was secure from a possible Arab attack. In the same year (1090), Count Roger also occupied the Maltese Islands. Having reduced the Arabs to a state of

vassalage and having released the foreign Christian slaves, he returned to Sicily without even bothering to garrison his prize. In Malta, the Normans followed the same enlightened policy and although the Christian faith was regarded as the official religion, nobody was persecuted for their race or religious beliefs.

In 1127 Roger II, the son of Count Roger, led a second invasion of Malta. Having overrun the island, he placed it under the charge of a Norman governor and garrisoned the three castles then on the islands with Norman soldiers. The last Norman king died without a male heir however, and the new masters of the Maltese islands came, in turn, from the ruling houses of Germany, France and Spain: the Swabians (1194); the Angevins (1268); the Aragonese (1283) and finally, the Castilians

(1410). When the Norman Period came to an end, the Fief of Malta was granted to loyal servants of the Sicilian Crown. These Counts, or Marquises of Malta, as these nobles were styled, looked on the fief simply as an investment – a source for the collection of taxes and something to be bartered or sold when no longer viable.

The last feudal lord of Malta, Don Gonsalvo Monroy, was expelled from the island following a revolt. By this time, the Maltese were thoroughly Christianized and houses of the great Religious Orders were being established on the Islands: the Franciscans (1370); the Carmelites (1418); the Augustinians (1450); the Dominicans (1466); and the Minor Observants (1492), while the Benedictine Sisters settled in Mdina in 1497.

◀ Mdina (Medina)

THE KNIGHTS OF ST JOHN

As a military order, the Knights took part in the Crusades, but when Acre fell in 1291, they were driven off from their last stronghold in the Holy Land.

After a short stay in Cyprus, the Knights, with the assistance of the Genoese, occupied Rhodes. This was to be their home for the next two hundred years until they were forced to leave the island by Sultan Suleiman.

After wandering for seven years, the Knights and the refugees from Rhodes who had attached themselves to them, were offered the island of Malta as a home by the Holy Roman Emperor, Charles V. To the relief of the Maltese Nobles, the Knights decided that Mdina, the capital city, was too far inland, and they set about establishing themselves in the small village that had grown up behind the old Castell'a Mare. In Birgu, the Knights organized themselves along the lines they had evolved during their stay in Rhodes. The Order could be described as a multi-national force divided into Languages according to the nationality of its members. These languages, or tongues, were: Auvergne, Provence, France, Aragon, Castile, England, Germany and Italy. Each language had its own Auberge, or headquarters, as well as a specific duty traditionally assigned to it, and each language was also responsible for the defence of a particular post, such as a section of a bastion or tower.

As if to prove the inadequacy of the defences of the islands, in 1547, and again in 1551, the Turks launched two attacks against them, the latter being the particularly calamitous. Ravaging the Maltese countryside and ignoring the fortified towns, the Turks then turned their attention to the island of Gozo and carried away the entire population into slavery. These attacks pushed the Knights into feverish activity to improve the defences of the islands in anticipation of another attack.

✳ THE GREAT SIEGE

"Nothing is better known than the siege of Malta," wrote Voltaire two hundred years after the event, and for the Maltese people today the statement still holds true.

The bare bones of the narrative are as follows. On the 18th May 1565, the Ottoman Turks and their allies pitted 48,000 of their best troops against the islands with the intention of invading them, and afterwards make a thrust into Southern Europe by way of Sicily and Italy. Against them some 8,000 men were drawn up: 540 Knights; 4,000 Maltese; and the rest made up of Spanish and Italian mercenaries. Landing unopposed, the first objective of the Turks was to secure a safe anchorage for their large fleet, and with

that in mind, they launched their attack on St Elmo. After a heroic resistance of thirty-one days, the fort succumbed to the massive bombardment and continuous attacks of the Turks.

After the fort had been seized, the Ottomans turned their attention to the two badly fortified towns overlooking the harbour, Birgu and Senglea. Subjected to ceaseless bombardment, and repulsing attack after attack behind the crumbling walls, against all odds the Christian forces kept the enemy at bay until a small relief force of some 8,000 troops arrived from Sicily. The Maltese people were able to drive back the Turks and so save themselves.

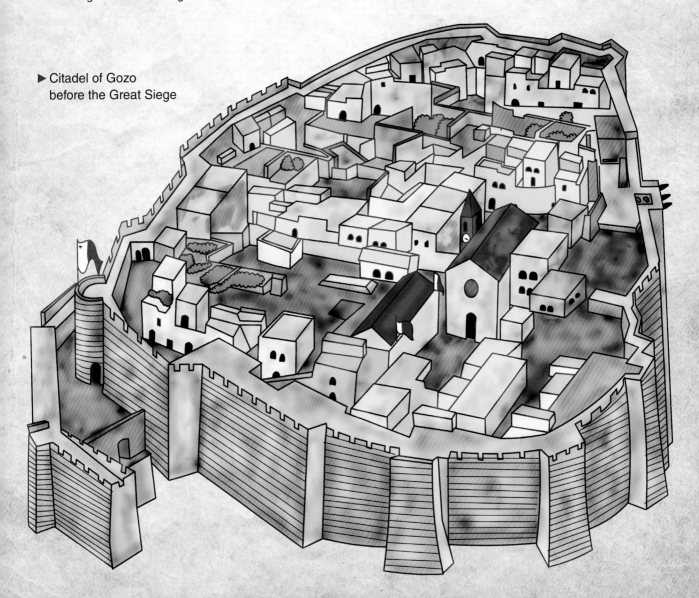

▶ Citadel of Gozo
before the Great Siege

✠ THE FOUNDATION OF VALLETTA

The idea of fortifying the rocky and steep-sided Mount Sciberras had occurred to the Knights on their arrival in 1530, but because time was not on their side, they limited themselves to building a fort at its furthest tip instead.

If other Grand Masters had studied the possibilities of such a project, La Valette was obsessed with the idea. As soon as he was elected Grand Master in 1557, he invited foreign military engineers to prepare the plans, but the Great Siege put a stop to that. No sooner was the siege over than the plans for the fortress city were again revived, but as a first step the ill-fated Fort St Elmo was

▼ One of the Great Siege frescoes by Matteo Perez d' Aleccio at the Palace State rooms.

DIMOSTRAZIONE DI TUTTE LE BATTERIE

at once rebuilt. Pope Pius IV sent his military engineer, Francesco Laparelli, and the planning of the new city started in earnest. When Laparelli departed from the Island, he left his Maltese assistant, Gerolamo Cassar, to continue the work he had started.

La Valette died in 1568 and was buried in the church of Our Lady of Victories, the first building to be erected inside the new city.

✠ THE FALL OF THE ORDER

When the Order made Malta its home, for the first time the rulers of the Maltese lived on the Island itself, and wealth was brought to the Island, rather than extracted from it. However, the finances of the Order were now in a precarious situation.

Unemployment was rife and poverty was widespread. Towards the end of the 18th century, the situation the Order was in was deteriorating. In France, where most of its overseas property lay, the possessions of the order were taken over by the Republican Government. French refugees, fleeing to Malta from the revolution, were an added drain on the treasury of the Order. While the last Grand Master of Malta, Ferdinand von Hompesch, was being elected, Napoleon was making his plans to take over the island.

✠ THE FRENCH

Napoleon's capture of Malta in June 1798 cannot be counted as one of his military triumphs. The Grand Master surrendered without offering any resistance and Napoleon made his grand entry into Valletta while within a week, Von Hompesch, accompanied by a few knights, left the island. The Maltese felt that they had been let down by the Order, but before they could attempt any resistance they were talked into submission by the Bishop. Maltese that had served in the Order's army and navy were recruited into the French Republican forces, and other regiments were raised for garrison duties on the island itself. After stripping the palaces, Auberges, and other buildings of everything of value, Napoleon, conveniently forgetting his promises, next turned his attention to the churches. Only such articles that were indispensable for the "exercise of the cult" were left, while all other valuables were removed and priceless works of art in gold and silver were melted down into ingots.

Nominally, the Order had held the Island of Malta in fief from the King of Sicily (since 1735 Sicily had been amalgamated with the State of Naples and was then known as the Kingdom of the Two Sicilies), and it was to the King of the Two Sicilies that the Maltese now turned for aid and protection. At the same time, deputies were despatched to seek aid from the allies of the King, the British.

A small number of British troops were landed and the French in Mdina surrendered in October 1798, the Sicilian flag being hoist on the ramparts. As the siege wore on, the French who were penned in the fortifications round the harbour were prevented from receiving aid due to the British blockade, though the Maltese, by this time aided by Italian and British troops, did not have the means to assault the formidable bastions. The French, by now exhausted, were ready to capitulate but Napoleon's troops proudly refused to submit to Maltese rebels. The British, on the other hand, anxious to deploy their troops and warships in other theatres of war, were eager to speed up the surrender of the French in Malta, which took place in 1800.

▲ Napoleon Bonaparte by Jacques-Louis David

THE BRITISH

Once the French were expelled from the island, the British were not so much interested in possessing Malta, as in keeping the French out. In fact, with the Treaty of Amiens (1802) that brought hostilities between Britain and France to an end, it was decided that Malta should be returned to a reformed Order of St John under the protection of the Kingdom of the Two Sicilies and that her neutrality would be guaranteed by all the Great Powers.

With the British in command of the sea, all mercantile shipping was obliged to call at the harbour of Valletta and before long, the Maltese Islands became the most important centre of trade in thc Mediterranean. Under the Treaty of Paris (1814), the island was confirmed as a British possession. Agriculture was encouraged to make the Island Fortress as self-sufficient as possible and potato cultivation, now a major agricultural export, was introduced.

The ever-present problem of water supply also received urgent attention. Prosperity brought about a rapid rise in the population and emigration was actively encouraged to ease the burden on the economy of the Fortress. Italian political refugees of the Risorgimento sought refuge in Malta and the example of these Italian patriots had the effect of further fanning the flames of Maltese nationalism. At the insistence of the Maltese population, a Council of Government was set up in 1835.

The military worth of Malta and its islands was to be demonstrated during the Crimean War (1854-56) when the Island Fortress became a rear base for the departure of troops and a receiving station for casualties.

Imperial policy dictated that Britain take Malta under full protection and anglicize, as far as possible, the local population. The First World War placed Malta on a war footing and, as had happened in the Crimean War sixty years earlier, Malta was to provide harbour and dockyard facilities to the Allied Navies, while her contribution in the cause of sick and wounded soldiers hospitalized on the island earned Malta the title "Nurse of the Mediterranean". A National Assembly was set up to make proposals for a new constitution. During one of the public meetings of this Assembly, held on the 7th June 1919, the crowd grew hostile and troops were called out to restore order. With the new Constitution approved in 1921, Malta was, at last, to be granted self-government with responsibility for all internal affairs. The British Government retained control over Defence, Foreign Affairs, and Immigration.

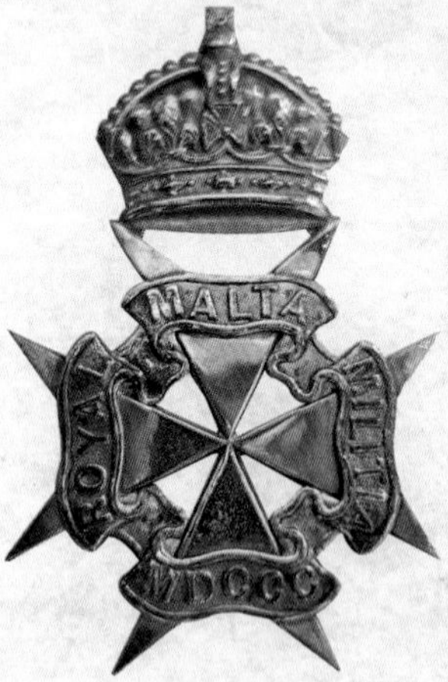

THE PATH TO INDEPENDENCE

For the Maltese people the path to independence was neither smooth nor straight. By the time Malta was granted self-government in 1921, the political factions could be classified into three main groups: the pro-British group, the pro-Italian group and the Labour Party, a newcomer in the political scene.

In the troubles that followed, elections were suspended and in 1930, the Constitution was withdrawn. In the subsequent election the pro-Italian party, with the support of the Church, won at the polls with a great majority. In the political storm that followed, the Constitution was again suspended and one year later Malta reverted to colonial rule. The British Government was now in sole control of the island. By the time the next constitution was granted, World War II was under way.

▼ The George Cross was awarded to the island of Malta by King George VI

When Italy allied itself to Germany, Malta was thrown into the front line. In June 1941 Hitler attacked Russia and the Luftwaffe in Sicily diverted most of its planes to the front. The air raids on Malta eased, but did not cease entirely. At the same time, having reinforcements, Malta took to the offensive.

On the 26th July 1941, the only seaborne attack directed against the Grand Harbour by Italian E-boats was brave and dashing, but unsuccessful. When the Luftwaffe returned to Sicily in full complement, the bombing commenced once more and Malta was again thrown on the defensive. A third of the anti- aircraft crews were Maltese and they soon made a name for themselves with their bravery and efficiency. On 15th April 1942 King George VI awarded the George Cross Medal to "...the brave people of the Island Fortress of Malta".

If the morale of Malta's defenders was high, the material resources of the island were low; with supply ships being intercepted and destroyed by Axis aircraft and submarines. By July 1942, the supply of vital provisions was calculated to last two weeks. Although badly mauled, the "Santa Maria Convoy" limped into the Grand Harbour on 15th August of that year and the situation was saved. In July 1943, using Malta as an advance base, the Allies invaded Sicily and the war moved away from the island. True to their promise made during the War, the British restored self-government. Fresh elections were held and the pro-Italian exiles were repatriated.

As most of the inhabitants were homeless, reconstruction was the first priority of the newly elected Labour Government, but social conditions were also improved. In the area around the docks especially, the trade union movement grew in strength as workers everywhere were becoming conscious of their rights. Three years later, following a split in the Labour Party, the Nationalist Party headed a Coalition Government and this party now strove to obtain Dominion status for the island. Originally the party representing the intelligentsia, it now attracted numerous workers within its ranks. On the return of the Labour Party to office, a request for integration was made to the British Government with Maltese representation at Westminster. When the British began to appear reluctant after evincing an initial interest, the Labour Party went to the other extreme and insisted on Independence. The acrimonies that followed were to cost the Labour Party many votes.

The Constitutional Party, the original pro- British party, died a natural death, its mission having been accomplished. In the wake of fresh elections and confirmed by a referendum, Malta achieved Independence within the Commonwealth on 21st September 1964 with the Queen of England as the nominal Queen of Malta. Under the next Labour Government, Malta was declared a Republic with Sir Anthony Mamo as its first President. On 31st March 1979, with the termination of the Military Base Agreement, the last British serviceman left the island and Malta entered into a self-imposed state of neutrality. Since 1st May 2004, Malta has been a member of the European Union.

▲ The Maltese Flag

MALTA

Malta is the main, and the largest island of the Maltese archipelago. The capital of the Republic of Malta, Valletta, is located here as are other important cities such as Mdina, the old capital, and Rabat. The island is densely packed with buildings, especially in the area around Valletta, and it is often difficult to know where the boundaries between the various cities and towns lie.

◀ Xarolla Windmill, Żurrieq

▲ Gardjola, Overlooking Grand Harbour

Despite the lack of boundaries between villages and towns, each area has its own characteristics. Even different dialects exist between the south and north of Malta, and the other island, Gozo.

There are interesting archaeological sites on Malta providing evidence of ancient, highly-developed civilizations that dwelt here in prehistoric times.

In addition, one finds the important monuments, churches and fortifications built by the Knights of the Order of St John, present on the island for about three centuries.

Malta is also noted for its connection with St Paul, who lived here for three months following a shipwreck during his voyage to Rome.

Malta is rather flat (the highest point reaches only 258 metres) and the terrain consists of limestone and clay. The coastline is high and rocky to the southwest while to the east there are numerous bays and inlets such as Marsaxlokk and the Grand Harbour. To the north instead, there are sandy beaches where one can spend relaxing days by the sea. Lastly, various places in the area around Valletta provide entertainment for lovers of nightlife, the best known of which is St Julian's.

VALLETTA

When Grand Master Jean Parisot de la Valette laid the foundation stone of Humilissima Civitas Valletta, the last thing that he had in mind was a city of fine palaces. Valletta was intended as a fortress to protect the two harbours on either side of the rocky peninsula on which it was to be built.

◄ Valletta as seen from Sliema   ▲ The Renzo Piano Project

The first buildings to be erected were the Auberges: these were the headquarters of the different ethnic groups into which the Knights were divided. The National Library, the Bibliotheca, was the last building to have been built by the Order, having been finished in 1796. Valletta boasts three parish churches (two of these are the Church of St Paul's Shipwreck and that of Our Lady of Victories) and a host of others, but pride of place must go to St John's Co-Cathedral. The plain exterior of this edifice grossly belies its sumptuous interior. No space inside the Co-Cathedral is left unadorned, the walls are carved and gilded and the painted vaulted ceiling is a masterpiece by Mattia Preti, while four hundred slabs of marble pave the church.

In years gone by, people used to troop into Valletta every evening, filling the many cinemas, and crowding the coffee shops. Nowadays Valletta is a busy city full of offices, cafes, restaurants and cultural events.

Recently Valletta was announced as The European Capital of Culture for 2018. This prestigious title reflects the incredibly rich cultural heritage of this Baroque masterpiece.

▲ Upper *Barraka* Lift

▲ *Piazza Regina*

▲ St George's Square, Republic Street

✠ REPUBLIC STREET & MERCHANT STREET

Notable streets in Valletta include Republic Street, which is the main shopping street and probably the busiest. This street is longer, higher and broader than any other and has many bars, cafes and shops. The churches of St Barbara and St Francis are located here. Moreover, institutional buildings are also located in this street, including the Court and the Parliament. Its entrance has recently been renovated, as part of the Renzo Piano project in Valletta. Merchant Street, on the other hand, is famous for its daily morning market. Various items can be found in the market including food, detergents and clothes. These two parallel streets represent the main thoroughfares of the city. From early morning, both are extremely busy.

Valletta is adorned with various squares. St John's Square has many cafes and leads to the entrance of St John's Co-Cathedral. A newly refurbished square is St George's Square. Republic Square, also known as Pjazza Regina, is equally famous for open-air cafes or refreshments. Thus, strolling around the streets of Valletta, one can see that it is adorned with various relaxing squares and public gardens enjoying breath-taking views.

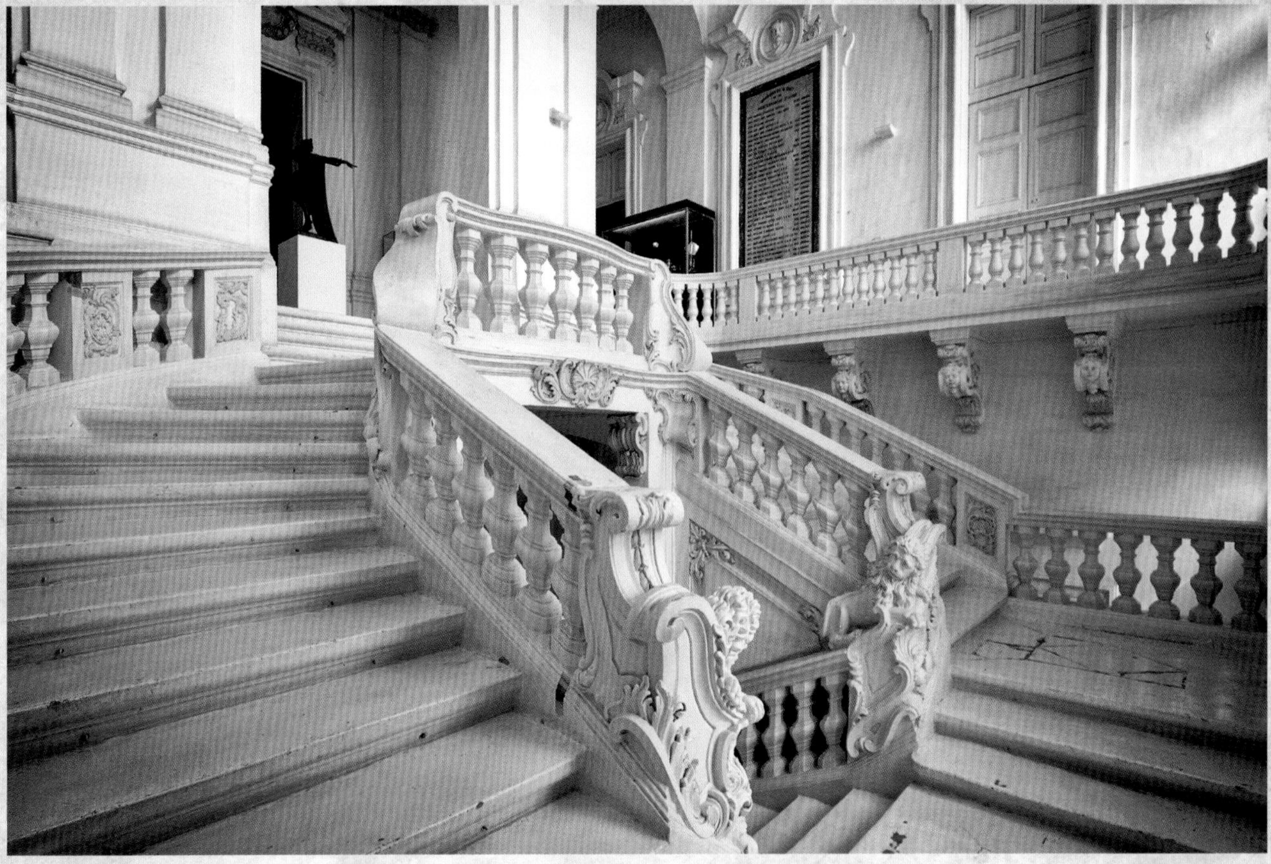

▲ The Salon in Admiralty House

NATIONAL MUSEUM OF FINE ARTS

Admiralty House, with the National Museum of Fine Arts is one of the palaces gracing South Street. This was one of the first buildings erected in Valletta, but it was rebuilt in its present form between 1761 and 1765. During the French occupation it was offered to the Bishop of Malta to be used as a seminary. On the capitulation of the French garrison, "Casa Miari" as the palace then became known, was occupied by the Commander of the Anglo - Maltese troops, Captain Alexander Ball.

In 1808, Louis Charles Viscount de Beaujolais, and his brother Louis Philippe, Duke of Orleans arrived on the island and were lodged in this palace; it was here that the Viscount de Beaujolais died. The palace was leased to the British naval authorities in 1821 and it remained the official residence of the Commander-in-Chief of the British Mediterranean Fleet. In 1961 it was handed over to the Maltese Government and in 1974 it was restored to its former glory and converted into a Museum of Fine Arts. It houses paintings, sculptures, furniture and objects associated with the Order of St John. Permanently displayed in this Museum are works by Reni, Valentini, Stomer, Preti, Tiepolo, Favray and Perugino. A section is especially reserved for works by Maltese artists.

▼ *Les Gavroches* by Antonio Sciortino

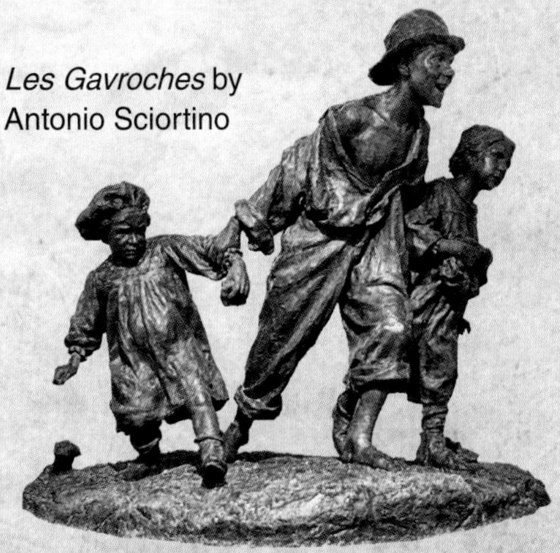

AERIAL
VALLETTA

✠ TEATRU MANOEL

The Theatre was built in 1731 by Antonio Manoel de Vilhena, Grand Master of the Knights of Malta at the time. He commissioned and personally funded the construction of this central building to keep the young knights of the Order out of mischief but also to provide the general public with "honest entertainment". This motto, "ad honestam populi oblectationem" is inscribed above the main entrance to the theatre. The first ever performance was Scipione Maffei's *La Merope* on 19th January 1732. *Teatru Manoel* was originally known as *Teatro Pubblico*. Under British rule it became the Theatre Royal, a title it lost in 1866 to its new rival, the much larger Royal Opera House, which was heavily damaged during World War II.

As Malta's national theatre, *The Manoel*, as it is affectionately referred to by locals, is one of the main contributors to the development of the local cultural scene. Its mission is to entertain, inform and educate, thereby enriching the cultural life of the audience. It is committed to the presentation of quality artistic productions, to the creation of new audiences for dance, drama and music and to provide a major platform for local and international artists.

ARMOURY MUSEUM

As presently displayed, the collection is small but interesting. On the death of a Knight, his armoury would become the property of the Order. The collection today contains over 5000 items dating from the 16th to the 18th century including the armoury of Alof de Wignacourt and of La Valette, two of the most important Grand Masters of the Order.

At the time of the arrival of the Order in Malta in 1530, the use of firearms was rapidly revolutionizing warfare – the Great Siege was fought largely with artillery and arquebuses but armour still had its uses – a century later breastplates and shields were still being tested against firearms, and in the Armoury there are several examples with dents in them to prove that they were "bullet-proof".

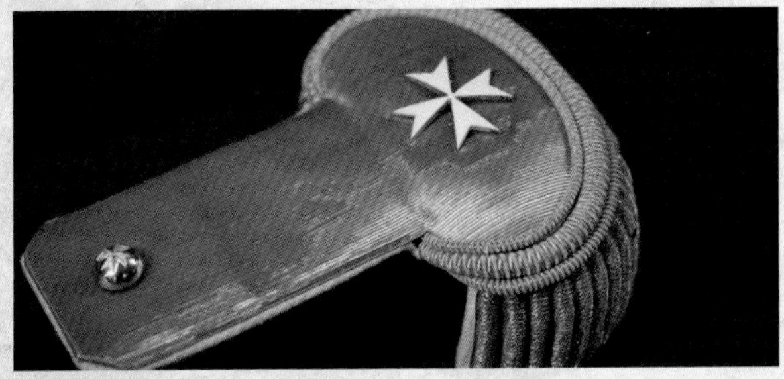

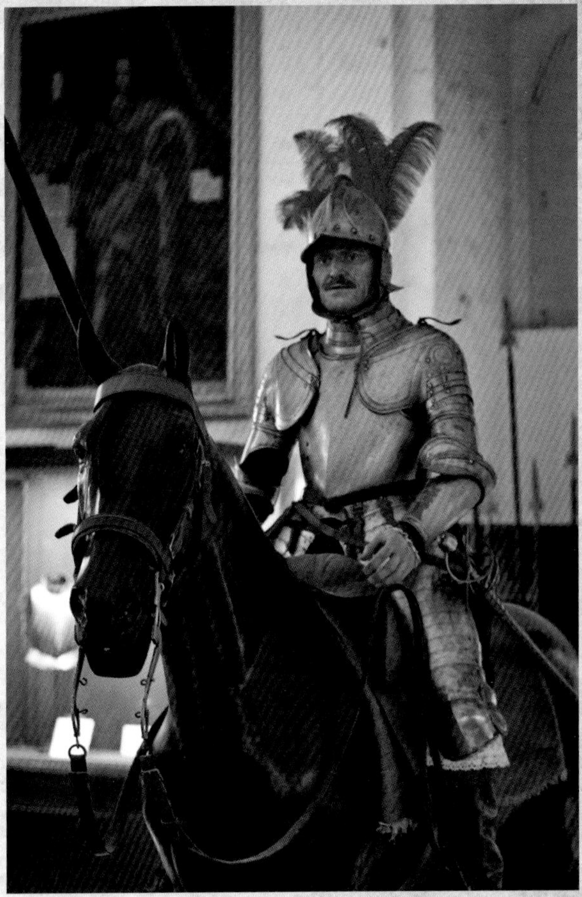

◄▲▼ Knights' armour displayed at the museum

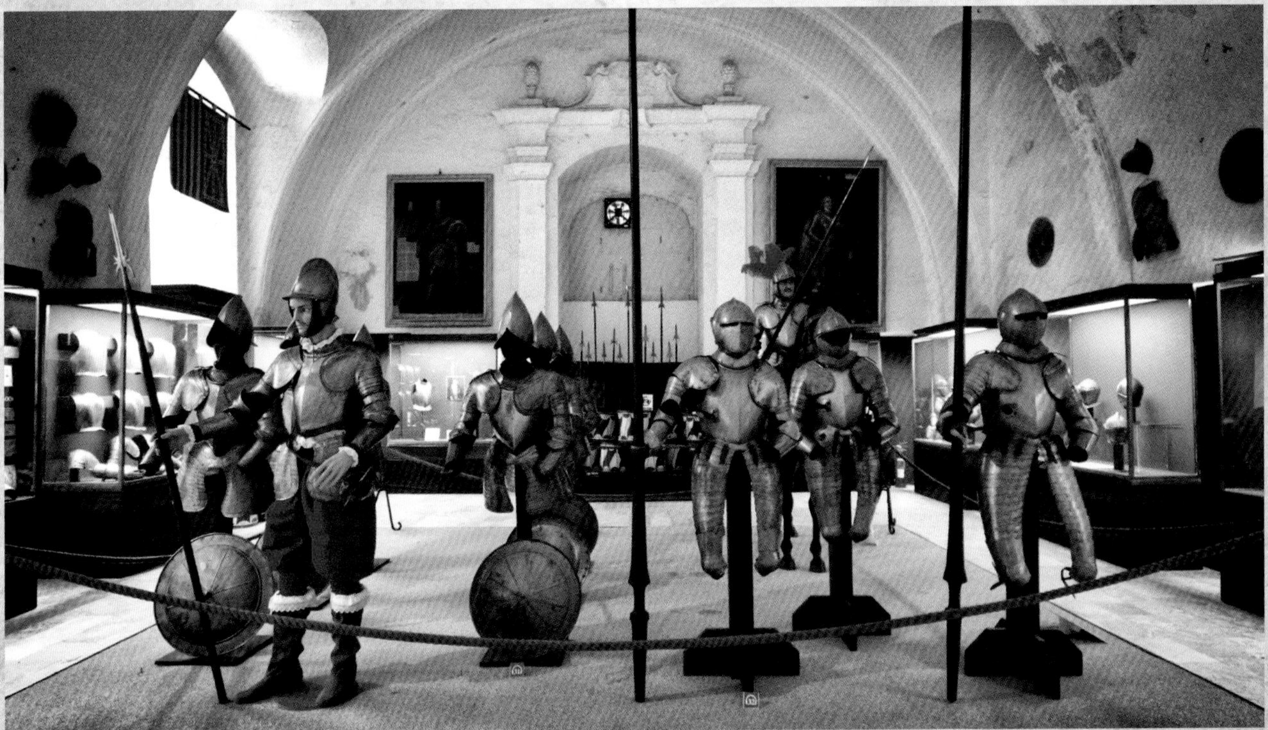

✳ THE GRAND MASTERS' PALACE

Valletta is a city of palaces but for the Maltese, the Grand Masters' Palace is known simply as *il-Palazz*; the Palace.

In its finished form, the Palace is built on two floors and occupies an entire block. Three of the doorways lead to a spacious courtyard while another portal and a gate lead to a smaller courtyard on a slightly higher level. The larger of the two courtyards is known as the Neptune Courtyard after the bronze statue of the god there. The smaller courtyard – the Prince Alfred Courtyard – is named after one of Queen Victoria's sons to commemorate his visit to Malta in 1858. However, this courtyard is better known as that of Pinto's Clock.

As in Renaissance palaces in Italy, the most important floor was the first, the *Piano*

▼ The Palace Corridors

▲ The Main Entrance to the Palace

Nobile, the ground floor being used as stables, service quarters and stores. The Main Staircase leading up to the *Piano Nobile* was built by Grand Master Hughes de Loubenx Verdala, identified by the wolf in the coat of arms.

The right-hand passage leads to what used to be the seat of the House of Representatives. The lunettes over the windows in this passage are the work of Nicolò Nasoni da Siena. The corresponding works were painted by the Maltese artist Giovanni Bonello some hundred and sixty years later. Together, however, the two series are complementary and show Maltese and Gozitan landscapes as they appeared at the time.

The Tapestry Chamber in the Armoury Corridor is an impressive hall where the members of the Order sat in Council. Here one finds the priceless set of Gobelins

Tapestries that give the name to this chamber. These magnificent tapestries depict fauna and flora from three continents.

To the left of the lobby, at the top of the Main Staircase is another corridor, known as the Entrance Corridor. This too is decorated with paintings by Nicolò Nasoni, depicting scenes of naval battles between the Order's galleys and those of the Ottoman Turks, apparently a subject dear to the hearts of these seafaring knights.

The first door to the right of the lobby leads into the State Dining Room. The next door along the Entrance Corridor leads to the Hall of the Supreme Council, also known as the Throne Room. Like all the other ceilings of the *Piano Nobile*, the wooden ceiling of this hall is elaborately coffered and painted, but the item of greatest interest here is a frieze of twelve frescoes by Matteo Perez d'Aleccio who worked in Malta between 1576 and 1581.

Against the far end of the wall is the throne, occupied first by the Grand Masters and then by the British Governors. Across the hall and opposite the throne, a carved minstrels' gallery is set into the wall; this carved and painted gallery is said to have been part of the Order's flagship, the Great Carrack of Rhodes, one of the vessels that carried the Knights to Malta.

A door from the Throne Room leads to the Ambassadors' Room, also known as the Red Room because of the colour of the damask covering the walls.

A door from the Ambassadors' Room leads to the Paggeria; the Pages' Waiting Room. A door from the Pages' Waiting Room leads into a corridor that is at a right angle to the Entrance Corridor. This is known as the Prince of Wales Corridor in commemoration of a visit by King Edward VII, then Prince of Wales, in 1862.

▼ Knight's Armour in the Palace Corridors

THE GRAND MASTERS' PALACE

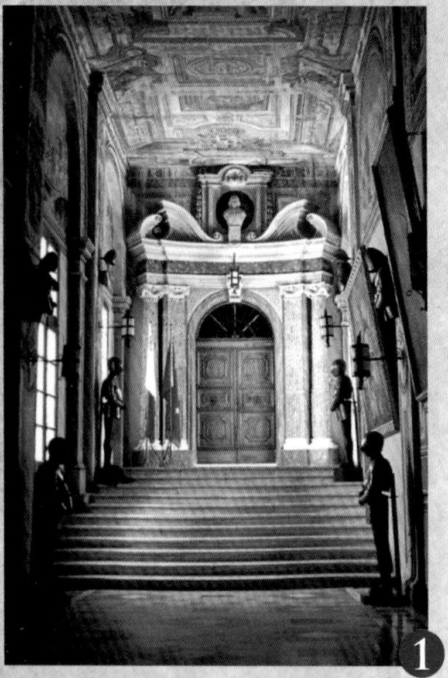

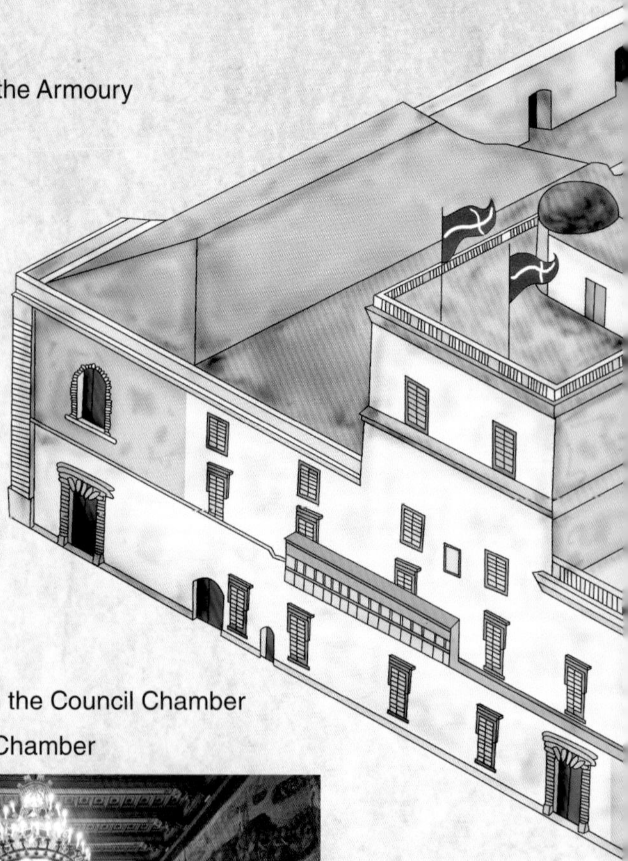

◄ Former Entrance to the Armoury

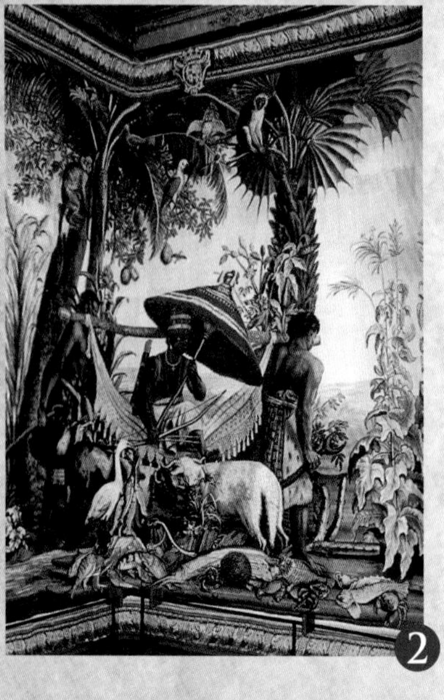

◄ Taperstry detail from the Council Chamber

▼ The Grand Council Chamber

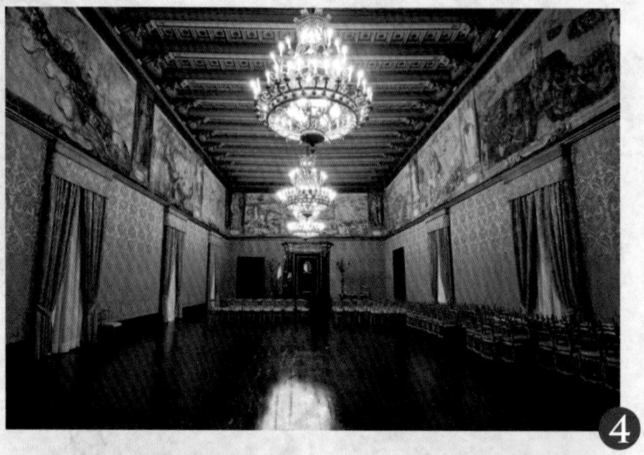

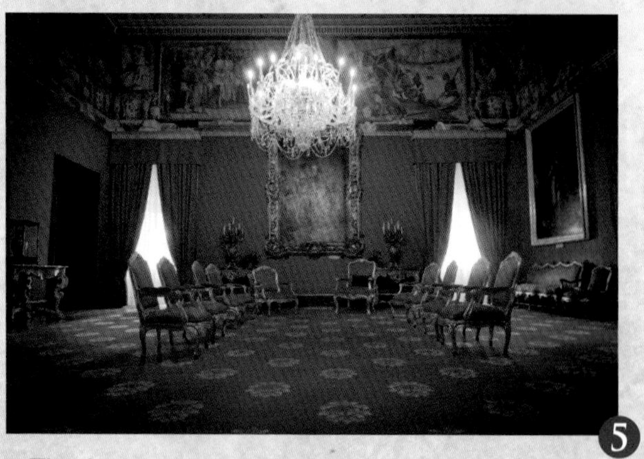

▲ The Ambassadors' Room

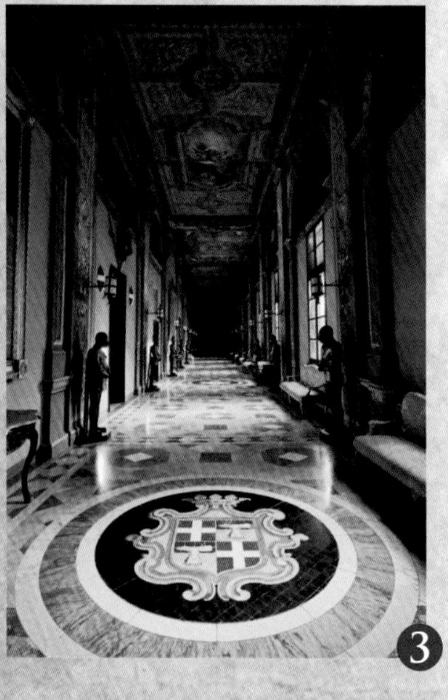

◄ The Corridor

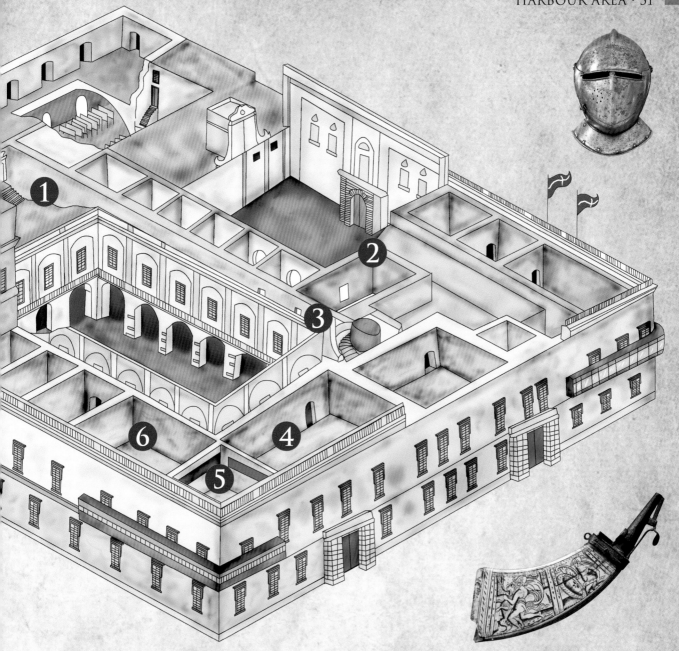

1

2

3

6

4

5

▼ The Pages' Room

6

CARAVAGGIO IN MALTA

When the famous and controversial painter became a fugitive from Papal authority for committing a murder in Rome, he chose Malta as his home. His enormous talent had secured the hospitality by the Knights of St John and later he was given a pardon by the Pope. Caravaggio produced a number of works for the Order and was eventually granted the title of "Knight of Grace" by the Order on 14th July 1608. On the 6th December, however, he was expelled following a violent brawl at Fort St Angelo, followed by his subsequent arrest with a Knight of higher rank. After this incident, Caravaggio did manage to escape to Sicily, but remained a fugitive, running from place to place, until his death two years later.

In 1608, commissioned by the Grand Master Alof de Wignacourt, he painted the "Beheading of St John the Baptist" to adorn the altar dedicated to the saint. The scene takes place in a prison as is evident from the faces of two

▲ *St.Jerome* by Caravaggio

prisoners watching from behind a grating. This is one of Caravaggio's most-prized works. Besides being known for its visual composition, dramatic palette and its blend of spectacle and piety, it is also famous as the only painting Caravaggio ever signed.

Opposite the Beheading is the striking "The St Jerome". This masterpiece shows the Doctor of the Church at work, writing in the shadow of death, represented by the skull on his writing-table, but spiritually protected by the distinct halo around his crown.

▼ The *Beheading of St.John the Baptist* by Caravaggio

✠ ST JOHN'S CO-CATHEDRAL

In 1573, Grand Master Jean de la Cassière authorized the construction of a conventual church of the Order of St John. It was completed in 1578 by the Maltese architect Gerolamo Cassar.

Its austere exterior gives no indication of the opulent and extravagant interior. A modest portico over the main door supports the balcony used by the Grand Master to present himself to the public after election.

The rectangular baroque interior was embellished by successive Grand Masters and further enriched by the "*Gioja*" or gift, which every Knight was bound by statute to give on admission to the Order.

Between 1662 and 1667, Mattia Preti "*Il Calabrese*" painted the life of St John the Baptist, patron saint of the Order, directly onto the primed stone of the ceiling. The altar is made of *Lapis lazuli* and other rare marbles. The Episcopal throne was originally reserved for the Grand Master. The side chapels were allotted to each of the "Languages" of the Order and the Grand Masters belonging to each particular language are buried here. The gates in the Chapel of the Holy Sacraments, like the candlesticks on the main altar, are made of silver.

The Grand Masters who died in Malta before the church was completed, are buried in the crypt, the most important sarcophagi being those of La Valette and La Cassière.

✠ ST JOHN'S CO-CATHEDRAL

▲ Mattia Preti, Vault Paintings

▲ Marble Tombstones, Floor

▶ Main Altar

3

▼ Our Lady of Philermos Chapel

4

▼ Flemish Tapestries

5

▼ Monuments to the Grand Masters

▼ A Chapel belonging to one of the Langues

✠ BARRAKKA GARDENS

The gardens, once private, are now open to the public. A fabulous view across the Grand Harbour and the Three Cities can be enjoyed from both gardens.

The Upper Gardens are enhanced by numerous statues including the group of *Les Gavroches* by the Maltese artist Antonio Sciortino. There is also a delightful little temple in the Lower Barrakka Gardens, dedicated to Alexander Ball who led the Maltese against the French.

✠ FORT ST ELMO

The Fort was built by the Knights in 1551 and was originally star-shaped. In 1565 during the great siege, the Fort fell to the Turks after 31 days.

After the defeat of the Turks, the Fort was given its present appearance by Laparelli. Later, further changes were made but these concerned the position of the weaponry, rather than the structure itself. In the 1970s this fort was used for the shooting of the movie Midnight Express.

✠ THE GRAND HARBOUR

The Grand Harbour is situated on an inlet four kilometres long. Boat trips around the port are available, and provide an introduction to the history of the island.

The Grand Harbour is guarded by Fort St Elmo and Fort Ricasoli. To the east, opposite the capital city, are Vittoriosa and Senglea. The Valletta waterfront has recently been restored and is now a popular area hosting various bars and restaurants.

◄ Siege Bell War Memorial from Lower Barrakka Garden

✽ THE NATIONAL MUSEUM OF ARCHEOLOGY

The museum contains a valuable collection of prehistoric artefacts such as pottery, statuettes and stone implements, as well as personal and other ornaments recovered from Malta's prehistoric and megalithic temple sites. Several table models of these temples are on permanent display and tomb furniture from the Punic and Roman periods are also exhibited.

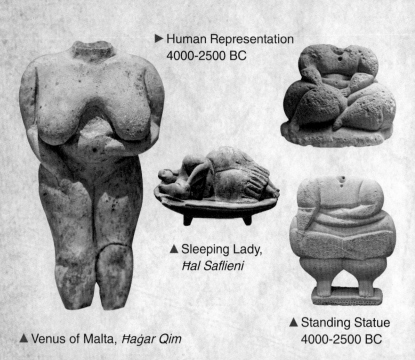

▶ Human Representation
4000-2500 BC

▲ Sleeping Lady,
Ħal Saflieni

▲ Venus of Malta, *Ħaġar Qim*

▲ Standing Statue
4000-2500 BC

✠ THE NATIONAL WAR MUSEUM

Housed inside Fort St Elmo is the National War Museum, where the George Cross given to Malta by King George VI during the Second World War, and the Gloucester Gladiator, one of the three airplanes active in the region at the beginning of the conflict, are exhibited.

▲ RAF & British Medals   ▲ RAF Pilot Gear

STREETS OF
VALLETTA

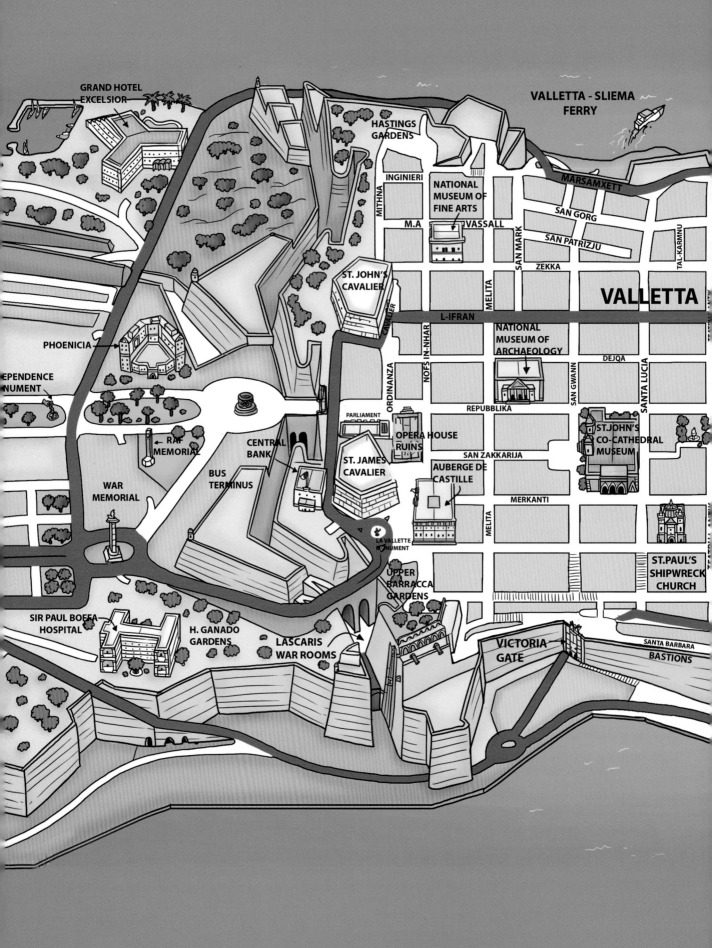

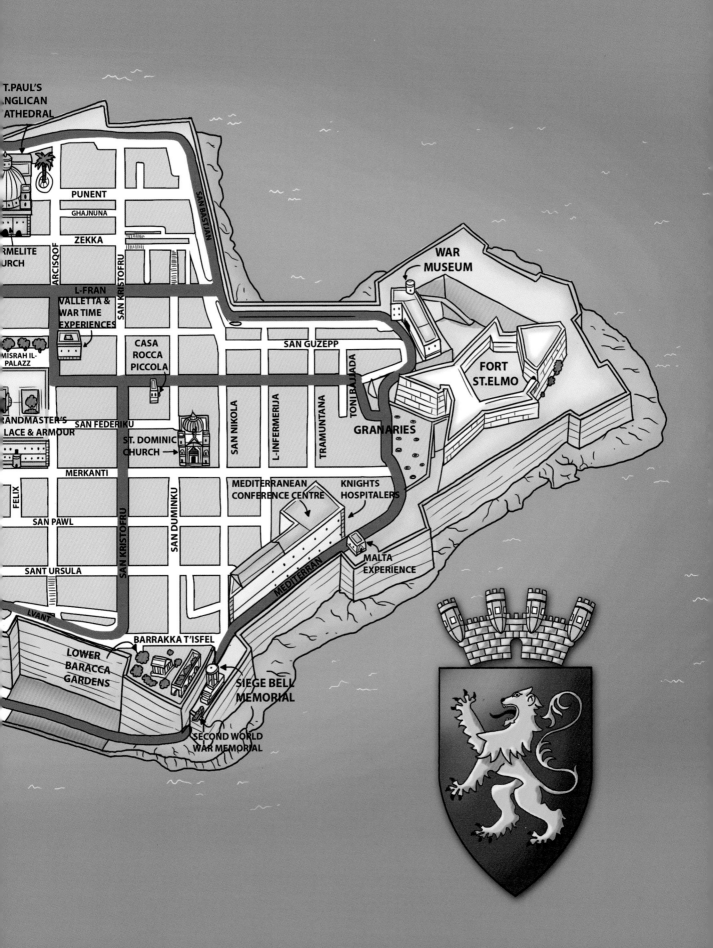

SLIEMA & ST JULIAN'S

Sliema and St Julian's are the main centres of tourism in Malta. Both towns provide all kinds of entertainment in the numerous hotels, restaurants, shops, bars and clubs.

Around the 1850s, Sliema became a summer resort for the well-to-do and, before long, the resort grew into a town. The rich built their villas on the ridge, away from the rougher area where the fisher folk lived. As the British servicemen left, the tourists moved in, and the houses of Sliema – both the villas and the hovels – were pulled down and blocks of flats and hotels appeared in their stead.

The promenade is probably the most densely populated area in the Island as strollers enjoy the sea-breezes in the cool of the summer evenings. St Julian's, its suburb, can claim an older ancestry. Originally, this hamlet sprang up around the old chapel dedicated to St Julian, patron saint of hunting (first built in 1580, but many times rebuilt).

The hunting lodges of the Knights have all disappeared except for that of Bali' Spinola who gave his name to the environs of the fishing harbour of St Julian's.

Where the old hunting lodges once were there are now the numerous hotels, restaurants and pubs that make St Julian's the most bustling and popular tourist resort in Malta, especially with the younger set.

PACEVILLE

Paceville developed during the 1930s as a district of St Julian's and today is the centre of Malta's nightlife. The suburb, situated on a hill between Spinola Bay and St George's Bay, is packed with numerous restaurants, discotheques and bars. Paceville also has an elegant Casino. Night owls will find plenty of entertainment here.

▶ Tigne Point (Top)
Balluta Bay (Centre)
Portomaso (Bottom)

▼ Spinola Bay

A NIGHT IN
PACEVILLE

THE THREE CITIES

Collectively known as the Three Cities, the towns by the harbour have, in fact, several names, though Birgu, Bormla and Isla are those by which they are most commonly known.

◀ Naval Bakery Clock Tower at Birgu Waterfront

▲ Aerial view of the Three Cities

Originally, Birgu (now Vittoriosa) was a small fishing village sheltering behind a castle of unknown antiquity that stood at the very tip of the peninsula. The castle, known as the *Castrum Maris*, or *Castell'a Mare,* had a measure of autonomy and was independent of the Università; the municipal council with its seat in Mdina.

On their arrival in 1530, the Knights decided to settle in Birgu; in the Fort, as Mdina was too far inland. They immediately set about protecting the hamlet with bastions. *Castell'a Mare* was strengthened and separated from Birgu by a ditch.

Not long afterwards, the adjacent peninsula, then uninhabited and known as l'Isla was likewise protected by bastions and by the time Claude de la Sengle was Grand Master it was sufficiently inhabited to merit the name of "Città Senglea" named, of course, after the Grand Master.

During the Great Siege of 1565 the inhabitants of Birgu and Senglea showed such outstanding courage that the two towns received the honorific titles of Città Vittoriosa (the Victorious City), and Città Invicta (the Unconquered City) respectively. The conurbation that linked Vittoriosa and Senglea was named Bormla (now Cospicua).

Merchants of several nationalities lived in the Three Cities and traded in slaves and other merchandise acquired by the corsairs and galleys of the Order. The cosmopolitan character of the Three Cities can still be seen: there are more "foreign" Maltese surnames in this part of the island than in any other.

Under the British rule, the Three Cities were a hive of activity as the Grand Harbour became the home base of the British Mediterranean Fleet, and at the same time, several rich Maltese ship-owning families settled in Birgu and Senglea. Being in close proximity to military installations, the Three Cities suffered terribly as a result of enemy bombing during World War II; Senglea in particular.

With the granting of Independence and the subsequent closing down of the military base (a *tableau* in bronze commemorates the farewell ceremony), oil tankers and freighters have replaced destroyers and cruisers in the dockyards.

Birgu, despite the bombardment, still has a lot to offer the visitor, such as a number of 16th century houses in which the Knights

made their abode on arrival: the Inquisitor's Palace, the magnificent Church of St Lawrence and the Maritime Museum. Built in 1660, the Inquisitor's Palace is one of the very few remaining examples in Europe of this particular architectural style and has probably survived due to the fact that throughout its five centuries of history it has always hosted high-ranking officials.

The Palace is an architectural masterpiece and now houses the Museum of Ethnography. The Church of St Lawrence was built over an older medieval church. It was destroyed by a fire but completely rebuilt in 1681 by Lorenzo Gafà. The two towers are later additions, however; the one on the left dates from the 18th century, while the other is 20th century. Exhibited in the Maritime Museum are models of ships, paintings, nautical instruments and arms illustrating Malta's seafaring history. Two rooms are also dedicated to the history of the navy of the Knights of Saint John and the British navy. For the energetic, a walk around the bastions of Senglea with a camera can be rewarding.

✚ THE SOUTH

MARSAXLOKK

Marsaxlokk, the harbour to the southeast, is now a small but picturesque harbour where the brightly-coloured fishing boats ride at anchor and where the wives of the fishermen knot nylon string bags for the tourists.

▲ Amateur Fisherman

▼ *Luzzu* Traditional Boat

A short distance from this village is the archaeological site of Tas-Silġ, still in the process of being excavated. The remains of Late Neolithic megalithic buildings have been found here, greatly modified by superimposed Punic and Byzantine structures; here too are the only remains of a mosque to be found on the island. Norman coins have also been found at Tas-Silġ.

To prevent the landing of corsairs in the harbour, the Fort San Luċjan was erected at its entrance by the Order. Used as a munitions depot during World War II, it now houses the Marine Research Centre.

Marsaxlokk Bay, of which the fishing harbour of Marsaxlokk forms part, is now being converted into a port for container ships.

MARKETS

Street markets are an important part of village life in the southern part of Malta, being held on a weekly basis and attracting both locals and foreign visitors. A popular market held in the south of Malta is the fish market in Marsaxlokk, which is well known for its freshness and variety, including traditional goods such as honey, goats' cheese and wine. Another popular Sunday market is held in Birgu and it is particularly interesting for the sale of antiques, collectables and other second-hand items.

WIED IŻ-ŻURRIEQ, THE BLUE GROTTO & DINGLI CLIFFS

The western coast of Malta is steep and precipitous but in places, clefts in the cliffs slope down to sea level. One such cleft is Wied iż-Żurrieq. This narrow arm of the sea provides anchorage for boats in calm weather. At the first sign of a storm, the boats are winched up a steep slipway and landed.

The boats at Wied iż-Żurrieq were, and still are, used for fishing. However, the fishermen are now discovering that it is more lucrative to take visitors to the nearby Blue Grotto. The presence of this deep sea-cave, in which the depths are of an unbelievably intense blue, has long been known to the fisher folk. During World War II, when an air-raid alarm was sounded, the people here took to their boats and rowed into the cave for safety.

North of the Blue Grotto are the magnificent Dingli Cliffs. Stretching for some 5 km, the cliffs rise to 250 m above sea level. At some points, the cliffs jut out directly into the sea, though at others they form small plains that are often cultivated. The cliffs provide a wonderful panorama.

✠ ḤAĠAR QIM & MNAJDRA

This Copper Age temple (Ħaġar Qim) was originally built in about 2700 B.C. but even then, it underwent several modifications. For some unknown reasons the axis of the first structure was altered and the temple itself was extended several times. The kind of stone used in the building of this temple (Globigerina Limestone) is rather soft and relatively simple to work. It is possibly for this reason that there are several "porthole" openings in Ħaġar Qim. A monolith on the outside of the temple wall has been tentatively interpreted as evidence of phallic worship. A pillar "altar" with an unusual palm frond decorative carving has been found in this temple, but not in any other. It is possible that this pillar was not originally part of the temple furniture and was placed there later.

Perhaps having learned that Globigerina Limestone does not resist bad weather, the builders of Mnajdra constructed this temple out of the harder Coralline Limestone which, however, was difficult to work with. The interior walls were faced with a softer kind of limestone.

The best preserved of the three Mnajdra temples is interesting because of the secret chambers that are hidden inside the thickness of its walls. These chambers communicate with the temple proper through the use of holes bored into the wall. It is surmised that statues of gods or goddesses could have been placed in front of these holes and the "priest" hiding in the oracle chamber was the voice of the deity as this "spoke" to the faithful. A healing cult may well have been practised in this temple as a number of baked-clay models of parts of the human body, showing symptoms of disease, have been found here.

✠ TARXIEN TEMPLES

In no other site in Malta is the evolution of prehistoric temple building better exemplified than it is at the megalithic temples of Tarxien. The earliest temples, now unfortunately in a vestige state, go back to around 2200 B.C., while the most recent of the four temples appeared in a burst of splendour some four hundred years later.

The spiral, as a decorative motif, is found in many places in Europe from the North Atlantic seaboard to the Aegean. The ones at Tarxien however, might have been invented, or at least developed, independently. What was probably the most colossal stone sculpture then in existence has been found inside the temples: originally 2.5 metres in height, the statue, presumably representing a Mother Goddess, has been broken in half and the top part is missing. There is a lot of conjecture about the significance of the statues of the "Fat Ladies" found in most of the Maltese temples. It is possible that they are examples of female fertility deities prevalent throughout the lands bordering the Mediterranean.

✠ GĦAR DALAM

In the era when the Maltese Islands were an extension of the Italian mainland, animals like elephants, hippos, deer and foxes roamed the land. With the rising of the sea-level, or the sinking of the land, or both, the islands were separated from the landmass and these animals were marooned. This took place in the Quaternary Era, some 10,000 years ago, and not during the Pliocene, five million to one million years ago, as was once thought to have been the case. In time these stranded animals gradually evolved into an island sub-race resulting in a degeneration in some of the species. Fossil bones of animals have been discovered in caves and fissures in various parts of the island, but the largest concentration to be discovered so far is that at Għar Dalam. In 1917, two human molars were found in this cave and, at the time of their discovery were believed to be those of Neanderthal Man. However, these molars have now been assigned to a much later period and it can be assumed that when the animals died, and their bones were carried into Għar Dalam by the action of flowing water, man had not yet arrived in Malta. Stone Age man did use Għar Dalam as his abode around 4000 B.C. but by this time, these animals had become extinct in the Maltese Islands.

ĦAL SAFLIENI HYPOGEUM

The Ħal Saflieni Hypogeum was created between 4100 and 2500 B.C. and discovered in 1902 by a group of labourers who were building a house. The Hypogeum consists of three levels, though only the first can be visited.

The structure was used both as a burial place (the remains of about 7000 people have been found here) and as a temple where fertility rites took place, as the characteristics of the numerous statues found here would seem to indicate (the figure, for example, of the "Sleeping Woman" housed in the National Archaeological Museum of Valletta).

The Chamber of the Oracle is particularly interesting: the roof is decorated with a tree motif representing the Tree of Life and a small niche amplifies the voice, also creating an echo. It was probably from here that the priests enunciated their oracles.

MOSTA

Mosta is roughly in the geographical centre of the island of Malta and, in times gone by, it was considered to be far enough inland to be relatively safe from corsair attacks.

◄ Main Altar at the Mosta Dome   ▲ Mosta Dome

Given its position, Mosta is an important crossroad lying on the route for those travelling from the south and the east towards the north of the island.

The chief attraction is now the monumental church, dedicated to the Assumption and called St Mary's, with its circular design inspired by the Pantheon in Rome. Its dome is the third largest in Europe, the two other domes being in Rome and in London. The building was started in 1833 and the church was consecrated in 1871; it was built around and over an earlier church which continued to be used during the period when work was in progress. In today's machine-age, it might seem that construction took an exceedingly long time, but it should be remembered that work on the church was done on a voluntary basis, in the little spare time that the labourers had at their disposal. Like many other of the old churches in Malta therefore, this is a true monument of faith.

In 1942 a thousand pound bomb penetrated St Mary's, piercing the dome and rolling through the interior without exploding.

MDINA

The Arabs divided the Roman town of Melita in two parts: the citadel, which they named Mdina (the Town) and the rest of the old settlement, which they named Rabat (the Suburb), names by which they are still known.

◀ Mdina Cathedral   ▲ Main Gate

During the medieval period Mdina was the seat of the Municipal government and administrative centre as well as a mustering station for the militia at the approach of the enemy.

At this time too, a number of religious orders built their monasteries outside the walls of Mdina and established themselves at Rabat and its surroundings.

When the Order of the Knights arrived in 1530, they realized they would be better served if they established themselves by the harbour where their galleys lay at anchor, and

as a result of this decision, they left Mdina and its inhabitants undisturbed.

When Valletta was built and eventually became the capital of the Maltese Islands in 1571, Mdina was relegated to being the *Città Vecchia* (the Old City). Some of the inhabitants of Mdina did migrate to the new city but among those who stayed on were the aristocratic families of Malta who still occupied their ancestral homes there; this had the fortunate effect of preserving a number of old 14th and 15th century houses and palaces. The old Maltese aristocratic families owned large rural properties and from time immemorial the farmers came to Mdina to pay their yearly dues to these nobles on the traditional date of the *Mnarja* (an ancient harvest festival, Christianized into the feast of Saints Peter and Paul).

This feast was, and still is, celebrated under the trees of Malta's nearest thing to a forest, the Buskett. Here, in 1586, the Grand Masters built a hunting lodge and summer retreat known as Verdala Castle. Because Roman law forbade burials inside the city, the catacombs were located outside the walls of Melita (now Mdina) and here too, according to tradition, is the cave in which St Paul was kept prisoner for three months.

The Main Gate to the City was erected in 1724 by Grand Master De Vilhena, replacing an earlier drawbridge gate the outline of which, now walled up, is still visible some metres away to the right of the present gate. It is reached by a narrow stone bridge, over a moat dug out by the Arabs, and is decorated with stone trophies of arms supported by lions – the lion forms part of Grand Master Vilhena's escutcheon.

On the outside is a Latin inscription giving the date and some details of the building of the new gate. There is also a trophy beautifully carved in stone and decorated with martial and triumphal symbols and with the Grand Master's arms on white marble, surrounded by the coat-of-arms of the city of Mdina and those of Vilhena once more.

On the inside are the coats of arms of Antonio Inguanez and a Latin inscription that commemorates his action to quell a rebellion in 1428. Bas-relief carvings of stone recall the patron saints of the city: St Paul, St Publius and St Agatha. A headless Roman marble statue, now in the Museum of Roman Antiquities, was once encased in the wall of the main entrance.

There are many beautiful buildings and monuments in this small city, including in particular, the 18th century Vilhena Palace, now housing the Museum of Natural History, and the elegant palaces of Villegaignon Street, as well as of course, the impressive and austere Cathedral.

AERIAL
MDINA

✠ ST PAUL'S CATHEDRAL

According to tradition Malta's earliest Cathedral was dedicated to the Blessed Virgin Mother of God. This was dismantled in the Muslim period but reconstructed and rededicated to St Paul after the Norman conquest.

This old church was modified and enlarged several times. In 1419 a horizontal rectangular wing was added to the edifice. In 1626 Bishop Baldassarre Cagliares added a recess at the back and in 1679 Bishop Molina laid the first stone of the choir which was inaugurated on 28th June 1682. The terrible earthquake of 11th January 1693 destroyed the old Cathedral almost completely except for the sacristy and the newly constructed choir. The latter had already been decorated with a fine altarpiece, a painting representing St Paul's Conversion and a fresco depicting St Paul's Shipwreck, as well as five other works, all painted by Mattia Preti (1613-1699). These fortunately survived the earthquake.

Building of a larger Cathedral in the new baroque style was immediately taken in hand and entrusted to the Maltese architect Lorenzo Gafà who eleven years earlier had constructed the apse choir. There was no need for a new plan. Gafà had previously submitted the plan and wooden model for a church in the new baroque style and the Cathedral Chapter had examined and approved them on 18th May 1692, eight months before the earthquake took place.

The new Cathedral was completed and consecrated in October 1702 by Bishop Cocco Palmieri (1684-1713) whose coat-of-arms, along with those of the reigning Grand Master Fra Ramon Perellos (1697-1720) and of the City of Mdina, was placed on the façade over the main entrance.

✠ CATHEDRAL MUSEUM

The Cathedral Museum in Archbishop Square is an imposing baroque palace housing a fine collection of arts and archaeology as well as important archives.

The building, completed in 1744, was constructed as a Diocesan Seminary and served its purpose up to the first decade of the present century. It was then utilized by various ecclesiastical and educational institutions until on 5th January 1969 it was inaugurated by Sir Maurice Dorman, Governor General of Malta, as the Cathedral Museum. The bulk of the art collections result from a legacy by Count Saverio Marchese (1757-1833).

A newly opened large room on the right of the entrance serves for the temporary display of new acquisitions, but the room is also offered to local artists for exhibiting their latest works and for hosting one-man exhibitions.

RABAT

Both Rabat and Mdina are perched on a ridge dominating the whole expanse of the island and of the sea beyond. Both centres have been inhabited for thousands of years.

▲ Verdala Palace, Buskett

Rabat incorporates a good part of the old Roman city, which was reduced to its present dimensions by the Arabs. This explains how the sumptuous townhouse with its fine polychrome mosaic pavements once inside the Roman town of Melita, now forms part of Rabat as the Museum of Roman Antiquities.

The Rabat area is intimately connected to the introduction of Christianity to the islands: in 60 A.D. St Paul the Apostle, under arrest on his way to Rome and shipwrecked on the island, is said to have lived for three months in a cave within the ditch below the walls of the old Roman city. St Paul's Grotto, as it is now known, served as a centre for his activity in establishing a primitive Christian community.

Since then the area has been dedicated to St Paul and is overlooked by a church where an important cemetery was located in medieval times. Burial being prohibited inside the walls of the city, the area outside the ditch, from

St Paul's Grotto to Buskett, abounds with a concentration of hypogea – or burial places – of pagan, Jewish or Christian origin dug into the rock by the Phoenicians, Greeks, Romans and Byzantines. Their tombs contain a rich variety of architectural elements. The largest of these are the St Paul and the St Agatha complexes in the Ħal-Bajjada district.

Before the coming of the Knights, Rabat became the centre of various religious orders, which preferred to build their houses in a place not far from the capital city but at the same time sufficiently secluded for their monastic retreat. The Knights, concentrated in Vittoriosa and Valletta, erected very few buildings in Rabat and did little to embellish the area.

Today, besides schools and colleges, Rabat has various social and musical band clubs, a market that is very popular on Sunday mornings, and playing fields. The Rabat area is ideal for walks in the countryside.

✠ ST PAUL'S CHURCH & GROTTO

The main square of Rabat is dominated by the Church of St Paul. It stands on the site of the house of the Roman governor, Publius, who was converted to Christianity by St Paul.

The present church was designed by Francesco Buonamici, the architect who brought the Baroque style to Malta, and was built by Lorenzo Gafà between 1656 and 1681. The church is particularly noted for its

unusual façade with three portals. Inside are many works of art portraying scenes from the life of St Paul. Near the main entrance is a stairway leading to St Paul's Grotto, once the destination of frequent pilgrimages.

This is located in the heart of Rabat. St Paul is reputed to have sheltered here whilst in Malta, and stone from the cave was accorded miraculous powers.

✠ ROMAN VILLA – DOMUS ROMANA

The Roman Villa Museum covers the site of a rich and sumptuously decorated town house belonging to a wealthy person in Roman Malta. The site, discovered in 1881 and further excavated between 1920 and 1924, contains a number of remarkably fine mosaic polychrome pavements and some original architectural elements. A number of rooms were constructed to protect the mosaics and an upper hall was added to provide exhibition space and a suitable entrance. The porticoed new-classical façade was completed in 1925.

✳ THE CATACOMBS OF ST PAUL AND ST AGATHA

These catacombs are well worth a visit, and in summertime offer cool respite from the sun. There are pagan, Jewish and Christian catacombs with a wide variety of tomb types among the maze of passageways.

Note particularly the *agape* tables or *triclinia;* round tables hewn out of the rock where commemorative feasts are thought to have been held on the anniversaries of deaths.

ST PAUL'S BAY

✠

The area of St Paul's Bay is a haven for tourists, attracting both young and older holidaymakers. Even the locals look at this area as a holiday destination. Foreigners find it ironic, that in such a small sunny island there is a culture of having a summer home in this location.

◀ Bugibba Square

▲ Bugibba Jetty

The town of San Pawl il-Baħar has many reminders of its namesake – one of Christ's Apostles. Here one can find Għajn Rażul; the Apostle's Fount, at which the saint is reputed to have quenched his thirst following his shipwreck and the church at San Pawl Milqi, the place where St Paul was welcomed by Publius, the Roman Governor. A number of churches have been built successively on this last site and, significantly, at the lowest level of the archaeological site, Roman remains have come to light.

✠ BUGIBBA

Until just a few decades ago, Bugibba was a rocky and barren headland with no particular point of interest; at its tip is a small coastal garrison of the Order that surrounds an older watchtower. Today it is a tourist hub, bustling with activity especially in the summer months when the weather is at its best. Clubs, lidos & restaurants fill the promenade right up to Qawra.

✠ QAWRA

Qawra, a district of St Paul's Bay, is located on the northeast of the Maltese islands. Popular among tourists, it is home to many hotels and restaurants. Although there is no beach, many people swim and bathe off the rocks, which provide ample space for sunbathing. Along the coast there are many water-sport activities including banana boat rides and speedboat rides. Casinos, bars, and clubs are also a major part of this small town.

Recently a National Aquarium opened in the area. The aquarium has twenty-six tanks including a walk-through tunnel for adults and another one specially designed for children.

◄ St Paul's Islands from Bugibba Jetty

▲ National Aquarium

▼ Qawra Coastline

MĠARR

Mġarr, formerly known as _Mgiarro_, is a small town in the northwest of the mainland of Malta. Mġarr is a typical rural village situated in an isolated region, west of Mosta and is surrounded by rich farmland and vineyards.

▲ Mġarr Surroundings

Mġarr's history is that of a farming community patronised by several of the Mdina patrician families. Over time, land was split up and given to all descendants.

Mġarr today has grown quite large, though still considered a country town with fresh clean air away from the major industrial towns of Malta. Over the years, it has also built a reputation for being one of the best places where one can eat stewed rabbit and snails in garlic, considered as Maltese specialities. Most of these restaurants are situated around the Mġarr Parish Church. This church is known for its unusual egg-shaped dome.

Mġarr also has two important prehistoric sites - Ta' Ħaġrat, which is still in a good state of preservation, stands in a field near the village centre; the other site, Ta' Skorba, excavated in 1963, lies just outside the village.

▼ Ta Ħaġrat Temples

MELLIEĦA

The locality of Mellieħa has, through its sustainable initiatives succeeded in achieving the 2009 title of excellence.

Situated on a series of hills, Mellieħa is a town in the northwest of Malta. Its elevated position, 150metres above sea level, grants it magnificent views all round.

The surrounding areas are characterised by hills, valleys, large caves, sheltered areas, fertile soil and natural spring water. Nature is definitely the strongest attraction of this town - beautiful fertile valleys provide excellent country walks.

In the valley just beneath the church lies Malta's largest fresh water reservoir. This is a fresh water haven for migratory birds; in fact, it is a Bird Sanctuary. Further up from the reservoir, on a hill situated opposite the hill of the main village one finds the Red Tower.

▲ Sanctuary Chapel

▼ Red Tower

BEACHES & BAYS

Blessed with over 200 days of sunshine, the northern area offers some of the loveliest beaches one can find on the island. The most famous beaches of Malta are found on the western coast up to the furthest northern tip, Mellieha. The longest stretch of sand in all of Malta is here and the calm waters of the bay make it an ideal beach for families.

▲ ❈ GOLDEN BAY

This beach is one of the most equipped offering the beach reveller a variety of water sports, ice creams, and hot bodies. It is busy throughout the whole week and severely overcrowded on public holidays and Sundays.

▲ ✠ RIVIERA BAY

This beach is one of the most idyllic and less frequented due to the long staircase leading to it. Notwithstanding the effort that one has to make to reach this beach, it is definitely worth it.

▼ ✠ ĠNEJNA BAY

Ġnejna itself is a picturesque beach offering interesting walks on both sides of the bay. Although the beach is busy one can escape the chaos by finding a spot on the coast.

AERIAL
BEACHES

▼ ✠ ANCHOR BAY

Anchor Bay is where the clear waters are full of fish, making it a perfect spot for divers. Robert Altman made his film Popeye starring Robin Williams in this bay.

▲ ✠ PARADISE BAY

Situated very close to the Ċirkewwa ferry terminal this beautiful beach enjoys views of Gozo and very clean and crystal-like waters.

▲ ✠ MELLIEĦA BAY

Also known as Għadira Bay to locals, this long stretch of beach is situated just in front of a natural bird reserve. Although very popular with Maltese and tourists alike, it is mostly a family beach due to its shallow waters.

THE ISLAND OF COMINO

The little island of Comino is named after a plant that grows on its shingly earth: the cumin seed. The famous Blue Lagoon here attracts thousands to its crystal waters.

For long periods of its history, Comino was an unsafe place in which to live. Nevertheless, people did inhabit this tiny island on and off, and the population figures fluctuate from nil to sparse. In 1416, the Maltese petitioned the Aragonese king, Alphonse V, to build a tower on Comino as a deterrent to the corsairs who made it their base, but the people of the island had to wait two hundred years before work was taken in hand. Eventually the Tower of Comino was finished under grand Master Alof de Wignacourt in 1618.

Despite the protection of the tower, people were wary of making Comino their home and the ancient church here was, in fact, deconsecrated in 1667 as being derelict. In 1716 the church was repaired and

re-consecrated, and by this time the island had been repopulated to some extent. With its handful of resident families and a single hotel, Comino, even now, has an air of a forsaken but beautiful island.

✳ BLUE LAGOON

The main attraction of Comino is the Blue Lagoon on the west coast of the island. The crystalline waters lapping the sparkling white sand beach are perfect for a swim and for snorkelling.

Across the small sandy beach off the main island is the small islet of Cominotto. Here another sandy patch sits a few metres away from a cave that leads to the open sea. The crossing to Cominotto can be done by swimming across the lagoon or by ferry.

GOZO

What awaits is a world apart. A quieter, more secluded and relaxed way of life with a still thriving agricultural and fishing industry.

◀ Citadel, Rabat   ▲ Rural Gozo

Malta's smaller sister island is different in that it is more fertile, more picturesque, and far more unspoilt; but what makes Gozo so markedly different from Malta are the Gozitans.

These frugal and tough people seem to be proof against any diversity; their character is tempered by privations and constant danger and, as a result of their frequent ordeals, they and their descendants have emerged strong and resilient. Malta and Gozo share the same history and historical remains which are duplicated in the two islands, but Gozo has had more than its share of misfortunes. Largely undefended, the island has many times been devastated by pirate attacks and on one occasion, the entire population was carried away into slavery.

When Gozitans had advance warning of an impending invasion, such as the Great Siege, some of them sought refuge in the better-fortified towns of Malta and some of the elderly were evacuated to Sicily, but they always returned home as soon as it was safe for them to do so. Gozitans ransomed from slavery also returned home, never deciding or desiring to settle in a safer place. Gozitan emigrants who become wealthy in the countries of their adoption likewise return home and build grand houses for themselves as evidence of their success.

Perhaps what makes Gozo special is the love and quiet pride of its inhabitants for their homeland. This pride is reflected, among other things, in the size and beauty of their churches.

VICTORIA

Also referred to by the Gozitans, as Rabat, Victoria is the main town in Gozo. The old city and the more modern area are intertwined.

It is in the centre of the island and has been the capital of Gozo probably from Roman times. Nothing structurally very old has survived but in the haphazard, twisting lanes and alley-ways of the town, splendid balconies and grand palaces revealing features of local architecture are still to be seen. Today Victoria is very popular among tourists & Maltese who visit the sister island for weekend breaks.

✳ IT-TOKK

The area has probably always been the centre and the marketplace of Victoria and still is today. In the morning, It-Tokk is bristling with activity. In the side streets round the square one can buy the delicious Gozo nougat, the *bankuncini* (almond based cakes) and the *pasti tas-salib* which are Gozo's sweet specialities.

✳ ST GEORGE'S CHURCH

St George's Parish covers almost half of Victoria. This church was built in the 1670s and suffered severe damage in the earthquake of 1693. A new façade was built in 1818. The dome and the aisles are of recent construction.

There are many works of art in this church, which include the paintings of the dome and ceiling by Gian Battista Conti of Rome and other paintings by Giuseppe Cali, Stefano Erardi and Mattia Preti.

The area over which the church is built is of considerable archaeological interest, dating at least to the Roman period.

THE CITADEL

The Citadel is a historic, fortified medina that lies in the heart of Victoria, Gozo. The northern part of the Citadel now lies in ruins, while the southern section where the cathedral is located is intact. The walls were recently restored to their former glory.

The Citadel is built on one of the many flat-topped hills in the centre of Gozo. Its origins can be traced to the late Middle Ages. At one time, the entire population of Gozo was obliged to take shelter within these walls after sunset. The walls themselves date back from the 16th to the 18th century. Most of the buildings inside the Citadel are in ruins but the Old Courts of Law and the Old Governor's Palace are still being used as the Law Courts of Gozo. There are also the Old Prisons and the Armoury of the Knights, the Archaeological, Natural History and Folklore Museums.

The Cathedral, together with the Bishop's Palace and the Cathedral Museum, dominates the Citadel.

✠ THE CATHEDRAL

The Cathedral, designed by the Maltese architect Lorenzo Gafà in the form of a Latin cross was built between 1697 and 1711 on the site of an older church. Inside, one's attention is drawn instantly to the flat *trompe l'oeil* ceiling depicting the interior of a dome, painted by Antonio Manuele of Messina in 1739. There are paintings by the Maltese Giuseppe Hyzler, Michele Busuttil and Tommaso Madiona.

Also of interest are the high altar inlaid with precious malachite and the baptismal font and its replica on either side of the main door, sculpted from blocks of Gozo onyx.

✳ FOLKLORE MUSEUM

This Museum is located in three late-medieval houses with Sicilian-influenced architectural features, in a small village, Għarb. Exhibits consist of agricultural implements, which include a mill for grinding corn, items related to the cotton industry, tools used in different crafts and some traditional costumes.

✳ ARCHAEOLOGICAL MUSEUM

All archaeological material found in Gozo is now exhibited in this 17th century house known as *Casa Bondi*. Of special interest are shards of the Għar Dalam period (5000 B.C.) found at Għajn Abdul, probably the oldest ever found in the Maltese islands, and the *Majmuna* tombstone, a beautiful marble inscription in Kufic characters dating to 1174 A.D.

Unique artefacts dating back to ▲ ▼ the Neolithic, Temple Period and Bronze Age (c. 5200-700 BC) found at the Stone Circle in Gozo

DWEJRA

Dwejra is an area of outstanding natural beauty on the north-western coast of Gozo. The area is a veritable museum of history, archaeology, natural history and geology.

✳ INLAND SEA

The Gozitans call it "Il-Qawra". This sea-filled basin is surrounded partly by the high cliffs and partly by a pebbly beach. The sea enters through a natural tunnel in the cliffs creating a vast pool of clear seawater. The sea here is warmer and is excellent for bathing, especially for children. It gets deeper as one nears the tunnel. It is recommended to walk in this area for there are other attractions worth visiting.

✳ FUNGUS ROCK

The locals call it il-Ġebla tal-Ġeneral as it is said that a Commander of the Order of St John discovered a shrub here that is known locally as *Għerq Sinjur.* The plant was protected by the Knights of St John as it was believed to possess great medicinal properties. In 1744, Grandmaster Pinto rendered the rock completely inaccessible and , until the middle of the last century a guardian watched over Fungus Rock.

✳ AZURE WINDOW

This is a massive natural archway rising out of the sea. The sea around it is intensely blue and provides some of the finest snorkel swimming in Malta and Gozo. There is an underwater cave close by, known as Il-Ħofra tal-Bedwin which is of exceptional beauty. One can take a trip in one of the small fishing boats of the Inland Sea round the Azure Window and the Fungus Rock.

SCENES OF
DWEJRA

✠ TA' PINU SANCTUARY

This is a national shrine and a centre of pilgrimage for both the Gozitans and the Maltese. On this spot there was a 16th century chapel dedicated to Our Lady of the Assumption, with an altarpiece painted by Amedeo Perugino in 1619.

The old chapel with the original painting can still be seen at the far end of the church where votive offerings are placed on either side of the shrine.

✠ XEWKIJA

The church of Xewkija is dedicated to St John the Baptist and its dome is one of the largest in the world. The dome of Xewkija was intended to be larger than that of the church of Mosta in Malta. In fact the dome in Xewkija is higher but the diameter is smaller. There are several good paintings in this church. Besides the altarpiece by Gioacchino Loretta, a pupil of Mattia Preti, there are three excellent works by Francesco Zahra, the most important Maltese painter of the 18th century.

✠ XAGĦRA

Xagħra became a parish in April 1688 together with Nadur, Sannat and Żebbuġ. The celebration in honour of the patron saint "Our Lady of Victories" is held every year with great pomp on 8th September.

The windmill was built in 1724 together with one at Nadur and another at Għarb, by the Portuguese Grandmaster Manoel de Vilhena.

ĠGANTIJA TEMPLES

The Ġgantija or, as it was commonly known in the past, "The Giants' Tower", is the best preserved and by far the most impressive prehistoric temple. It is probably the finest of all the ancient remains on these islands and can compare with Stonehenge for grandeur. It was uncovered in about 1826.

Ġgantija consists of two separate systems of courtyards that do not interconnect. They are known as the South Temple, which is bigger, earlier (c. 3600 B.C.) and better preserved, incorporating five large apses, and the North Temple which is smaller and a later addition (c. 3000 B.C.) with a four-apse structure. The great court of the South Temple measures twenty-three metres from apse to apse and the height of the wall here is preserved at eight metres, the highest of all the temples. The arch was not yet known in building and the span of the apses here is quite large for any conceivable stone roofing. Wood or animal hides might originally have been used as roofing material. Two kinds of stone were used in the construction; *tal-franka*, the soft stone mainly used inside as portals and floor slabs, and *tal-qawwi,* a harder stone that is mostly used for the general construction of the walls.

The interior of the walls was plastered and painted with red ochre. Traces of this have been found. The huge megaliths forming the outer wall (the largest weighing several tons) were built alternately, one horizontally and one upright. The space between the inner and outer walls is filled with rubble and earth and it is this system that has given the Ġgantija the necessary stability to withstand the depredations of more than 5000 years. The floor is partly covered with soft stone slabs and partly with *torba*, or beaten earth. Spiral and pitted designs decorate some of the soft stone slabs. One can hardly see the spirals today but when the site was uncovered, they were found in a good state of preservation, indicating that the temples had some kind of roofing protection while they were in use.

MARSALFORN

This is the most popular summer seaside resort in Gozo. During summer especially, the place is crowded with Gozitans and Maltese as well as tourists.

It started as a fishing village and the fishermen still keep their colourful boats in one sheltered corner of the bay.

Fresh fish is found in restaurants here throughout the year. During the hot weather, one can indulge in all kinds of aquatic sports. Bus transport to Victoria is in operation throughout the year at all times of the day and is more frequent during the summer.

Marsalforn has a small sandy beach, several hotels, guesthouses, holiday flats, good restaurants, many souvenir shops offering all kinds of Gozitan handicrafts, and other tourist amenities.

Round the western headland are the coves of Qbajjar, Xwejni and the fjord-like cove of Wied il-Għasri. On the eastern headland are Għar Qawqla, Għajn Barrani and Ramla Bay.

✠ XWEJNI

Xwejni Bay is easily reached through Marsalforn or Żebbuġ. There are two adjacent shallow bays with small pebbly beaches and rocky stretches leading into the deep blue sea. It is also a very popular diving spot, especially for beginners. It is a perfect spot to get away from busy Marsalforn.

A couple of fishing boats, boathouses, restaurants and bars are scattered along this beautiful coastline.

✠ SALT-PANS

Just past Xwejni Bay west of Marsalforn, the coast is dominated by the site of 350-year-old rock-cut saltpans. The Qbajjar Salt Pans are the biggest salt-works in Gozo, stretching over 3km long.

These salt pans are more than just scenic. Several tons of sea salt are produced there every year, continuing a centuries-old Gozitan tradition of sea-salt production.

✠ WIED IL-GĦASRI

Just down from Ta' Dbieġi Hill lies this beautiful valley which leads to a narrow creek known as Wied l-Għasri. Popular with swimmers and divers alike, this creek is known for clear waters and underwater caves.

Like Xwejni Bay, this narrow and secluded bay is also a haven for those who seek a quiet bathing area away from the bustling Marsalforn.

XLENDI

Xlendi, a village situated in the southwest of the island of Gozo, is another summer resort used by locals and tourists alike. Like all major tourist destinations, one can find all necessary tourist-oriented amenities, such as bars, restaurants, holiday flats and hotels.

Originally a fishing village, this beautiful inlet with a sandy beach has been recently transformed into a tourist haven. This is not surprising since Xlendi Bay is one of the most picturesque places on the island. Besides the beach and restaurants, one can enjoy beautiful walks along both sides of the bay. On the right side, the walk takes one up and down a rock-cut staircase into the cliffs, which eventually enters a cave that leads into the sea. To the left is a longer walk that also involves crossing the valley on an old stone bridge leading to the Xlendi tower and overlooking the saltpans. The tower guarding the mouth of the creek was built by Grandmaster Lascaris.

RAMLA BAY

Ramla il-Ħamra is a fine sandy beach on the north coast of Gozo, the best in both islands. Its name means "red sandy beach" and it is an excellent spot for swimming and a wonderful place for children to play. It is extremely popular with locals and tourists alike and in the busy summer months it can be difficult to find a spot on weekends.

There are those who argue that Ramla Bay is the best beach in all of the Maltese Islands. It is located at the end of a fertile valley, dotted with fields and terraced field walls situated on the north side of Gozo. Local farmers still tend gardens and orchards on both sides of the hills. The beach consists of a wide stretch of red sand. Its golden-reddish colour makes this beach different from all others in the Maltese Islands.

The surrounding undeveloped area is more than just sun and fun and there is myth and history here too.

The famous Calypso Cave overlooks the western side of the beach. This cave is said to be where Homer's sea nymph Odysseus, in her spell, overlooked the bay. Beneath the sand lie Roman remains and it is a *Natura 2000* site; a network of nature protection areas in the territory of the European Union

The beach is accessible from the village of Xagħra. Xagħra is located on one of the hills of Gozo and overlooks this valley. It would take around forty minutes on foot from Xagħra, though it is also reachable by bus.

BEACHES & CREEKS

The Gozitan island is full of small beaches and creeks that can be enjoyed during the summer months. Some are hard to find while others accessible only by sea. Here are two of the most cherished by the locals.

✠ HONDOQ IR-RUMMIEN

Accessible from the village of Qala this beach is located opposite the island of Comino, thus having beautiful views. Its small sandy beach and crystal-clear waters make it a popular swimming and barbeque spot for the locals.

✠ MĠARR IX-XINI

A gorgeous spot for swimming and snorkelling, this once-secluded inlet is increasingly popular and busy on weekends. A tiny pebbly beach at the head of the narrow sea inlet provides a gentle slope into the water. The bay attracts divers to several caves in the cliff faces and a nearby wreck of the ferryboat, Xlendi.

The Knights' watchtower that still guards the bay was built in 1661.

'LUZZU' THE MALTESE BOAT

These brightly-coloured boats, which derive from Phoenician vessels, are one of the symbols of Malta. The *Luzzu* is the traditional fishermen's boat. The *Dgħajsa* is similar to the Venetian *gondola*, but more colourful: it was used to transport both passengers and goods. Today the *Dgħajsa* can only be seen in the Grand Harbour. The bow of these vessels is decorated with the so-called "eyes of Osiris", a symbol of Phoenician origin that offers protection from all the dangers of the sea.

✠ EXPLORING THE DEPTHS

The Maltese archipelago, with its three principal islands (Malta, the largest; Comino, famous for its Blue Lagoon; and Gozo, the island of Calypso), is the ideal spot for underwater sports.

The waters of Malta's sea are among the most transparent and uncontaminated in the entire Mediterranean; the temperature varies between 23°C in the summer and 13°-15°C in winter. Diving in these waters is a unique and unforgettable experience among an exuberance of brightly-coloured marine flora and fauna. Many different species of fish are there for the seeing: sea bass, mullets, flying-fish, and the extremely rare Golden Perch, which risks extinction in the Mediterranean. However, fish watching is not an activity limited solely to summer. Even in the winter, the visitor will marvel at such magnificent examples as St Peter's fish, which swims close to shore. Both beginners and experienced divers will find many opportunities for underwater adventure in Malta and the chance to discover and explore natural ports, solitary bays, sheltered inlets, rocky cliffs, and even shipwrecks.

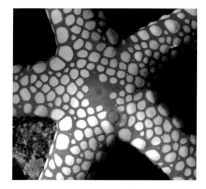

✠ MALTESE CRAFTS

The Maltese crafts tradition is a long and rich one. One of the best-known products is the bobbin, or pillow lace produced in Gozo and known for its intricate motifs. This type of handwork was introduced in the 17th century (even though it became well-established only in the 19th), when Genoese lace-makers came to the island. Maltese lace is therefore a variant of that produced in Genoa, even though it has many characteristic features, like inclusion of the Maltese Cross in the patterns. In the streets of Gozo, women still sit outside their homes to work with their pillows, pins and bobbins, just as they did many years ago. Another important craft is that of the Maltese silversmith, which developed during the era of the Knights and is held in high esteem all over the world even today. In the jewellery shops one will find beautiful gold and silver filigree work in both ancient and modern patterns. Malta's production of vases and multi-coloured glass is also highly renowned. The glass is still blown, hand-finished, and finally, painted in lively colours.

MUSIC & FOLKLORE

In Malta, one will find various opportunities to experience music rooted in a unique Mediterranean cultural heritage. Every village, town and city has at least one *banda* (brass & wind band) which provides the music entertainment during much of the local celebrations. The *banda* is particularly active during the summer months when most localities celebrate feasts dedicated to patron saints. The local folk ensemble *Nafra* is a popular item on Malta's cultural calendar featuring a contemporary fusion of authentic Maltese traditional instruments (bagpipe, cane flute, reed pipe, friction drum and other percussion instruments).

Malta also boasts its own Mediterranean folk music festival: *Għanafest*, held every June in the marvellous surroundings of Argotti Botanical Gardens in Floriana, with a programme of Maltese folksong, local bands and international guest artists.

✠ MALTESE CUISINE

Like every other Mediterranean country, Malta is blessed with fresh fish, tasty vegetables, sweet fruit and an abundance of lemons, olives, garlic and capers, mint, basil and much more sun soaked produce, enabling the Maltese cook to prepare the most appetising dishes whether traditional or innovative. Maltese dishes generally fall into one of two categories: the first being peasant cooking with its roots deep in the nation's history and probably little changed over the centuries. This is represented by the thick vegetable soups and stews, oven bakes of uncovered bread (ftira), goats' cheeses, and potatoes.

Other Maltese dishes have their counterparts throughout the Mediterranean and may be identified with various neighbours: *timpana* with the Sicilian *timballo*, and stuffed peppers and aubergines with the Levant. *Ħelwa* and *imqaret*, two favourite sweets, probably have Arabian origins. If the Maltese table has something to be proud of, it is undoubtedly its bread. The true Maltese *ħobża* is crisp and crunchy on the outside and beautifully light and soft on the inside. Apart from eating it in the usual ways, such as for sandwiches and as an accompaniment to one's meal or cheese, it is at its best as *Ħobż biż-żejt* – literally; bread with oil.

✠ MALTESE WINES

It is generally believed that the vine was introduced to Malta by the first Phoenician settlers. Except for the Arab period, viticulture in Malta flourished right up to the arrival of the British. By the end of the 19th century a replanting programme was started and viticulture flourished once again. Sizeable areas of land are now planted with international varieties such as Chardonnay and Merlot.

Like most other Mediterranean countries, Malta has ideal soil and climate conditions to grow excellent wines. Most traditional grape producers still grow local grape varieties (the white variety *Ghirgentina* and the red variety *Ġellewża*).

✠ CARNIVAL

One of the best periods of the year to visit Malta is Carnival time. The festivities reach their most frenetic in Valletta, but fascinating events are also held in the small towns of the other islands, and in particular in Nadur in Gozo. During Carnival, thousands of brightly dressed revellers invade the city streets to watch the parades with their fantastical floats. In Paceville one can party all night, moving from one club to another. Moreover, this week is undoubtedly the very best for making one's acquaintance with the vitality and festive spirit of the Maltese.

✠ NOSTALGIC MALTA

Although Malta has embraced modern development and in the last 20 years there has been a huge improvement in infrastructure, it is still in touch with the distant past and roots. This is visible in everyday life where it is not uncommon to spot old traditions still being practised.

✠ RURAL MALTA

It is a fact that Malta is very densely populated. However the coastlines, the north and the smaller islands still hold large patches of agricultural land. These locations provide exciting walks especially in Spring time when wild flowers bloom in the countryside.

RELIGIOUS MALTA

Religion is still the centre of most activity in Malta, although it is becoming more secular. Still every village has numerous churches and chapels. Even for non-believers some churches are works of art with amazing architecture and frescoes.